Also by Gwen Cooper

<u>YOU</u> are PAWSOME!

*75 Reasons Why Your Cats Love You,
and Why Loving Them Back Makes
You a Better Human*

GWEN COOPER

Contents

Foreword

C onsider this book my open love letter to all the cat people out there—people who are, in my own humble opinion, some of the very greatest humans alive.

Cat lovers tend to get a bad rap—"crazy cat lady" being among the most common pejoratives routinely flung at us—which I'm inclined to chalk up to the pure jealousy others feel upon observing some of the more admirable qualities our cats routinely bring out in us and then burnish to a high gloss: patience, generosity of spirit, the ability to love unselfishly without expecting "rewards," and our willingness to engage even our non-human companions with a spirit of mutual respect and understanding.

The aloofness our cats sometimes display makes us more open. Their innate snobbishness keeps us from believing ourselves to be *their* superiors and makes us all the more humble. Their inscrutability makes us smarter, master detectives skilled in the reading of nuance.

They also make us far more appreciative of the little things in life—of those small moments of grace that can infuse even ordinary of days with something akin to magic: the tiny paw laid gently atop our own hand; the affectionate brush of a tail against our shins; the sound of a soothing purr against our heart as we drift off to sleep.

Not to mention that cats—being nature's funniest animals, hands down—instill in us a wicked sense of humor.

Don't believe me? Keep reading. This book is chock-full of examples proving that cat lovers are indisputably, irrefutably, and one-hundred-and-one percent totally

PAWSOME!

You clean the litter box

There's no end to how feline-besotted the genuine cat lover is. So besotted that a true devotee can find the positive spin on even the most negative aspects of cat care—the extra expense of a home-visiting pet-sitter when you travel ("Totally worth it!"); the always-dicey experience of pilling a cat ("Muffy looks so cute wrapped in a 'kitty burrito!'"); and even cleaning up hairballs ("Bootsie and I *love* the smell of Nature's Miracle!").

But the one un-spinnable negative is cleaning out the litter box. Probably the best that can be said is that, under certain ideal circumstances—including use of a high-quality litter, and making sure not too much time has passed since the last cleaning—it's relatively painless.

Then there are those *other* times. You know what I'm talking about. Those times when the store was out of your favorite litter, so you had to make do with some cheap substitute that doesn't even *pretend* to cover up the odor, which probably explains why you waited a couple of days longer than usual to clean it out...

And now here it is, the middle of summer, 95 degrees outside and even hotter than that *inside*, the sweltering heat and cheap litter having caused the odor coming from the litter box to mutate into some hideous, nearly tangible, practically paranormal entity that surely no cat—certainly not *your* cat, who's so cute and tiny!—could possibly be responsible for. Suddenly you're Marlon Brando at the end of *Apocalypse Now*, helplessly repeating the only semi-coherent thought your mind is capable of forming:

The horror! The horror!

In the end, though, you roll up your sleeves, clothespin your nose, grab the scooper and a plastic bag, and head in there to do what you have to do like the brave, never-say-die soldier you are.

Because when the going gets tough, the tough get **PAWSOME!**

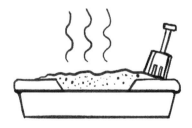

You're kind to other cats

It's an absolute given that *your* cat—the cat who's snuggled up to you right now—is the all-time greatest cat that has ever lived or will ever live at any place or time in the entire history of the world, forever and ever, amen.

You're especially likely to feel this way if you're someone who, in your young and misguided years, swore up and down that you didn't particularly like cats, and couldn't see what all the fuss was about—and yet you somehow ended up living with a cat eventually (perhaps when a cat-owning romantic partner moved in), at which point you fell like one of the pens your new feline friend delighted in pushing off counters, devolving into a cooing, crooning, *who's my mushy kitty???* fool.

But even if you think of yourself as a one-cat human, it's inevitable that the love of one cat will lead you to cast a kindlier eye on other cats as well. You may one day find yourself setting out a bowl of kibble to feed a hungry-looking neighborhood cat you previously wouldn't have thought twice about. You'll almost certainly end up giving an affectionate scritch to the friend's cat—wending his way around your ankles when you drop by for a visit—who, once upon a time, you would have completely ignored.

The point is that there's something about loving *a* cat that leads to loving *all* cats.

This means that loving a cat makes your heart grow larger. And everybody knows that having a bigger heart makes you a kinder and all-around better human being.

Just like we claimed right on the cover of this very book!

PAWSOME!

You're kind of a sucker, in the best possible way

They say that a sucker is born every minute. And the day *you* were born was a red-letter day in the history of sucker-dom.

Of *course* you're a sucker. You're one of the biggest suckers going! It takes little more than a hang-dog (or hang-*cat*) expression before you're feeding your own dinner to one of your pampered felines, or allowing him to continue his comfy snooze on your very favorite sweater, or pausing a movie just at that pivotal moment when the killer's about to be revealed so you can fish out the toy your now-crying kitty accidentally pushed under the sofa.

You keep a stash of treats in hiding places throughout the house so they're always close at hand, just in case a sweet and imploring tug of a paw against your pant-leg makes it clear that a treat must be dispensed right *now*. You move your cat's bed from place to place in your living room over the course of the day, so that it's always ideally situated in the sunniest spot. You might make your spouse and kids eat a dinner they're not overly thrilled with—but if the latest can you put down for Buttons is clearly bumming him out, a new and different flavor is never far behind.

In other words, you're a rube. It's no secret that your (kind of a) con-artist cat manages to bamboozle you daily with the greatest of ease.

When pressed on the subject, there's nothing you can do but admit it. Maybe it's all true. Maybe you actually *are* one of the biggest suckers who ever lived.

But as long as we're truth-telling—isn't that really just another way of saying you have a heart as big as all outdoors?

PAWSOME!

You let your cat lie on top of you

It could be 100 degrees outside. You could be full to bursting with that half (whole?) pizza you just consumed while re-watching Season 4 of *Game of Thrones* (#JusticeForSerPounce). Your cat could be a 25-lb. Maine Coon whose weight is a challenge for you to support, even under ideal circumstances.

No matter what, though—if Queeney wants to lie on your belly, then that's exactly what you're going to let Queeney do.

Is it uncomfortable? You betcha! But what's a little discomfort between very best friends?

And besides, it's incredibly flattering to know that your cat literally can't get close enough to you.

PAWSOME!

You open doors for your cat (and close them...and open them...)

What is it with cats and doors? My own cats have never met a closed door they could abide—even if that closed door leads into a room they have no desire to enter, or out of a room they have no desire to leave.

Capriciousness, thy name is cat.

There are any number of theories as to why cats abhor a closed door even more than nature supposedly abhors a vacuum. (Come to think of it, my cats aren't especially fond of the vacuum, either.) These include separation anxiety—the idea that your cat simply can't bear to be parted from you—a fear of being trapped in a room and at the mercy of potential predators when the door is closed, plain old curiosity (*say...what's behind that closed door anyway???*), and the maddeningly circular theory that states we've trained our cats to cry whenever they see a closed door by opening that door for them whenever they cry.

Heh.

I think we all know it's actually the other way around—that it's our cats who've trained *us* to do their bidding, and that when they demand we open a closed door or close an open door, they're simply exercising the prerogative that all masters have over their servants, i.e. the right to make arbitrary demands at all times and for no particular reason.

And while I'm not one to generally advocate for vassalage as a desirable state, I will say that acceding to my cats' more unreasonable demands with a kind of automatic patience has made me much more patient when, for instance, I'm filling out complicated health insurance forms, or dealing with an unreasonable desk clerk down at the DMV.

PAWSOME!

You read around your cat

A nd what is it with cats and newspapers?

Or cats and magazines?

Or cats and that book you have opened in front of you?

I used to have a hypothesis that your cat would see your eyes glued to a page and think something like, *There is NO WAY I'm letting her look at that magazine instead of at me!*, and would therefore resolve to get between *you* and *it* so as to effectively hijack your attention.

It was a good-enough theory, as such things go. But then I adopted a blind cat who very obviously couldn't see where my eyes were looking at any given moment (and didn't even have a working understanding of things like "eyes" and "looking"), and my blind cat *also* would instantly sprawl atop any magazine, newspaper, book, et cetera that I might have spread out on the table or floor before me.

Which means there's probably just something irresistible about the sensation of paper under their furry bellies that has your cats entranced.

Sure, you've been known to unceremoniously shove your cat off a book or newspaper so you can continue reading. But if you're anything like me (a born sucker, no doubt about it), you're just as apt to ask yourself, *Is there <u>really</u> anything entertaining and/or informative enough in these pages to justify disturbing Tabby when she's so comfy?*

And, after concluding that there almost certainly isn't, you content yourself with whatever fragments of sentences or paragraphs are visible around Tabby's fuzzy tummy—all the while assuring yourself that the sacrifice of reading material is a trifling thing when compared to the comfort of your beloved feline.

PAWSOME!

You work around your cat

W hile we're on the subject—what is it about cats and computers?

Or cats and desks?

Or cats and desk *chairs*?

Or cats and...well, you see where I'm going with this.

If it's something that's adjacent or essential to your work—something without which your work couldn't get done—there's a reasonably high chance your cat will be utterly fascinated by it.

Of course it's perfectly adorable and all that. But it doesn't change the fact that attempting to type on a keyboard that currently has a cat dancing up and down its keys—trying mightily to add her own imprint to your work reports by inserting an emphatic ***ad;lskfahk;h!*** for flourish—can make the actual *work* of getting your work done vexing, to say the least.

Look, you wouldn't be human if you didn't, on occasion, simply shoo your cat well clear of your workspace and get back down to business.

But you're probably just as apt to find yourself typing with a face-full of fur, hands spaced awkwardly on your keyboard as you try to edge around your cat's flapping tail to get a decent look at the screen in front of you.

That's because you're flexible, dexterous, and capable of effective multitasking. And also because nothing in your hierarchy of values—not even your work—comes ahead of your cat.

PAWSOME!

You sleep around your cat

It's an immutable law of physics that even a small, five-pound cat is somehow capable of taking up roughly the same amount of space in a bed as a six-foot-two, two-hundred-fifty-pound man.

I don't know how they manage it, either. As with so many things when it comes to cats, it's a mystery!

What isn't a mystery is why you choose to contort your body into pretzel-like formations that would be the envy of a Cirque du Soleil performer rather than kick Milo out of bed, or even so much as disturb his slumber.

You do it because, when it comes to your cats, you will *literally* give 'til it hurts. And being a giver is
PAWSOME!

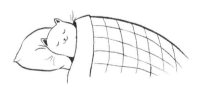

In games of cat and mouse, you're always "mouse"

When it comes to playing "cat and mouse," the rules are simple and exactly the same as the outcome, which is predetermined.

To wit: The cat gets the mouse.

The mouse is the eternal dupe of Fate, destined to be forever pounced upon. No matter how favorable the odds may appear at first, the deck is always stacked against him. Any hope that *this* face-off against the cat might be different is nothing more than a mirage floating on the horizon.

And yet, you always take the mouse role when playing a spirited game with your cat, wiggling fingers and toes under blankets or tablecloths or t-shirts or whatever else is handy. Never once is the game reversed. Never once, say, does your cat casually stroll past a bed *you're* hiding beneath, where *you* wait to leap out and pounce upon *him*.

In fact, your cat would likely be pretty resentful if you tried to turn the tables like that.

And even as your poor digits are bruised and torn for the umpteenth time by the teeth and claws of sweet little Fluffy, you smile courageously and remind yourself—even as your cat is using parts of your body as his own personal chew toys—that love and self-sacrifice are practically the same thing.

"It is a far, far more **PAWSOME** thing that I do than I have ever done..."

You berate yourself whenever you scold your cat

My cats are certifiable experts at making me feel guilty—although, given that I'll feel crushing guilt all on my own for forgetting to order a pizza with a well-done crust (my husband's preference), or for disturbing the robins and squirrels when I hang out in my back yard, making *me* feel guilty is clearly so easy as to be unworthy of my cats' prodigious talents. No need for them to open their eyes wide in a hangdog expression, or rub harder than usual against my leg in an attempt to remind me that their breakfast really *should* have been served twenty minutes ago. (*What kind of a monster makes helpless cats wait twenty minutes to be fed???*)

The worst, however, is when I find myself having to scold my cats for one reason or another—Clayton for having chewed the ear off of the cat-shaped wooden footrest I once brought home from a flea market. (Clayton likes to chew wood. Yeah...I don't get it, either.) Or Fanny for having pilfered a sample bag of dry kibble from the kitchen cabinet she *knows* she's not allowed to open.

Bad cat! I'll say in the sternest voice I can muster, accompanied by an equally stern wag of my finger. *That's very, very bad!*

But then, inevitably, I feel like an ogre. *They didn't <u>mean</u> to be bad,* I remind myself. *They're just doing what cats do.* Who do I think I am, anyway—the matron of some dour reform school for misbehaved cats? What do my poor kitties even have to look forward to in their listless little days, if not for whatever love and affection I dole out to them? Without that, their lives would be nothing but an endless, joyless cycle of naps and toys and back rubs, and thoughtfully prepared meals served punctually on time.

Quelle horreur! Who could endure such an existence?!

It's usually when I reach this point in my thoughts—and as a way of offsetting the intensity of my guilt—that I'll haul out the Temptations bag and dispense treats with a liberal hand. *Forgive me for having yelled at you!* I plead. *I didn't mean it! I'll do better next time!*

The irony of the whole thing is that—as their bored little faces are at pains to remind me—my cats, being cats, never actually gave a flip that I was angry at them in the first place.

PAWSOME!

You always put food in the bowl

Your cat might obsess over seemingly negligible taste differences between his favorite cat-food brand's Shredded Chicken Dinner (yum!) and their Minced Chicken Dinner (yuck!). Or maybe get incredibly fussy about another flavor of food he scarfed down with wild enthusiasm as recently as yesterday. Maybe even—heaven forfend!—you might oversleep one morning or get home late from work one evening, forcing your cat to wait a whole half-hour longer for his morning or evening repast than he's accustomed to waiting.

Bottom line, though? Your cat knows you're going to put *something* edible in that bowl Every. Damn. Day.

Even when the prices of gas and milk and bread and oranges rise to outrageous heights. Even when that year-end bonus your boss promised fails to materialize. Even when you lose your job altogether and have to resort to eating mayonnaise sandwiches without the mayonnaise. Come hell or high water, your cat has never once gone hungry.

Because you're reliable. Because you're *rugged*. Because you're
PAWSOME!

You give your cat adorable nicknames

Cats have their cat-specific rituals of inclusion—things like head-bonking, touching noses, and scent-marking your ankles. We humans have our own ways of letting the world know that our cats are family members, like including them in family photo portraits, getting a tattoo that features a cat's name or likeness, or writing our cats into our wills. (You may laugh, but do you know who would take your moggy in if something were to happen to you?)

For my money, though, one of the very best ways of letting your cats know they're equally valued family members is with the bestowing of a "family only" nickname.

My own cats have their real names, of course—the ones that go on their medical records and travel documents. But then there are the names known only to family and close friends. Clayton, for example, is known as Clayton, aka The Clayman, aka Claymation, aka "Littleman" (a running together of "little man," which somehow became a *thing* in our house when, after years of referring to Clayton as "my mushy little man," my husband decided to make the two words into a single sur-name-like nickname.)

And then there's his sister Fanny, aka Fandemonium, aka Fanny-cat, aka Fan-Fan, aka Miss Fanny Pants (I think I was originally going for a "fancy-pants" riff).

I won't share the family-only names my husband and I have for each other. Suffice it to say that everyone in our house—four-legged and two—has at least one nickname known only to those who reside within these four walls, and never uttered in front of outsiders.

Just like in your house! Which is how your cats know 100% for sure that they're completely official, much-beloved, fully vested members of the only club they're likely ever to think it worth their while to join.

PAWSOME!

You sing your cat silly love songs

Did you know that the word "kitty" can be substituted for the word "baby" in just about any song?

This is true in general, but particularly in the case of Motown classics, a happy happenstance I was thinking about just the other day while warbling an off-key rendition of The Miracles' "Ooo Kitty Kitty."

Who, for example, can refrain from crooning along with Martin Gaye's "Too Busy Thinking About My Kitty"? Or The Shirelles' "Kitty It's You"? I've been known to murder an interpretation of The Supremes' hit "Kitty Love" at dubiously appropriate times.

When it comes to my absolute favorite, though, it's a two-way tie between Ronnie Spector and The Ronnettes' "Be My Kitty" and "Kitty I Love You." (*Have I ever told you/ How good it feels to hold you?*)

Not that it ultimately matters what specific song you're singing to your rapt feline audience of one. The important thing is that your cat knows you're singing for him, and him alone.

Bonus points for working your cat's name into "The Name Game"! (*Patches, Patches, Bo-batches, bonana fanna fo-fatches...*)

PAWSOME!

You give your cat daily massages

A recent lower-back spasm was of such agonizing intensity that I found myself unable even to hobble as far as the nearest chiropractor—and so, for the first time in my life, I hired a massage therapist to come to my home.

My tripod cat, Clayton, stayed pretty close while the massage was going on—Clayton being a very "present" cat—and the massage therapist, a cat lover herself, remarked that he was clearly one of those cats who likes to "supervise" the humans around him.

That may very well be, but my suspicion is that Clayton wasn't trying to exercise his cat's prerogative of being in charge of all the people around him.

He was trying to figure out why *I* was the one getting the massage instead of *him*.

After all, a full-body rubdown is a cherished part of Clayton's daily ritual. If more than 24 hours passed without soothing, scratching fingers all down the length of his back, he'd surely feel that he'd been monstrously deprived.

Some people may have cats that like to "groom" them, as my cats occasionally do for me. But let's be honest: Most cats will simply accept your daily ministrations—the scratching, the rubbing, the massages—as no more than their due.

And you, upon seeing (and hearing!) your cat's purring pleasure—and even though you're on the giving rather than the receiving end of all this attention—are still likely to think that you're the one getting the better end of the deal.

PAWSOME!

You don't make your cat feel weird about being weird

It always gets my back up when I hear some non-cat person talking about how "weird" cats are. Scoop out a few litter-boxes and pay your dues like the rest of us, and then maybe—*maybe*—you'll be entitled to opine on the alleged "weirdness" of cats.

Since we're just talking amongst ourselves, though, we can be honest and admit it: Cats are kinda weird. They get all riled up for no apparent reason and chase invisible things up the walls and sleep in boxes that are WAY too small to be comfortable and chitter at birds outside and run away at top speed from their own poop like pooping was a crime and they're barely one step ahead of johnny law.

Those of us who love cats, however, know that variety is the spice of life. Truth be told, many of us are a bit on the odd side ourselves, which is why we actually like the "weirdness" in our cats.

In fact, we don't just like it—we love it! We love that each and every one of our cats has their own individual quirk, like only being willing to drink water out of *our* water glass, or leaving the same stuffed mouse on our pillow every night, or *constantly* showing us their butt. (Actually, that last one probably applies to all cats.)

Nobody ever attained greatness by being just like everybody else. And let me ask you this: Do you love the ones you love because they're so ordinary, or do you love them for the ways in which they're different and unique and stand out from the crowd?

Wouldn't it, in fact, be fair to say that noticing those differences in someone else is how love usually begins? And wouldn't it *also* be fair to say, then, that those of us who already have a propensity for appreciating a little bit of weirdness—the whole reason why we love our cats in the first place!—are somewhat likelier to be kind and accepting of others,  even (and especially!) if they're slightly on the odd side?

So there you have it: We embrace the weirdness in our cats without ever doing anything to squelch their unique personalities or make them feel self-conscious. We savor their little eccentricities through the eyes of a connoisseur, not the eyes of a conformist.

And it's exactly this tendency that makes us more loving, more open-hearted, and more accepting human beings in general.

PAWSOME!

You defend your cat against visitors who complain about cat hair

What's a cat-hating psychopath like *that* even doing in your house in the first place???
PAWSOME!

You find your cat's bloodlust adorable

If you had a relative or coworker who was always thinking about the violent murder of bunnies and songbirds, chances are you'd find that person kind of...icky. *I guess he* probably *won't murder me and stuff my corpse in a Dumpster,* you'd reassure yourself, right before asking HR to reassign you to some faraway cubicle, or scratching Cousin Creepy off the invite list for your wedding.

Personally, I'm a big fan of the various birds, bunnies, squirrels, butterflies, opossums, and other wildlife denizens who populate my back yard. I throw out nuts and seeds and little bits of bread on a regular basis, and I set out bowls of water when the weather is particularly dry. I had to wait nearly three months this year to get some much-needed professional yard work done—only to reschedule my long-awaited appointment when it finally arrived, because by then I had two little robin fledglings hopping around my back yard under the watchful eye of their *very* uptight mama, and the thought of their combined anxiety when faced with the deafening roar of weed whackers was enough to give *me* an anxiety attack.

I get a little over-invested in the birds and bunnies, is what I'm saying.

And yet, like the vast majority of cat-moms and dads, the sight of my cats crouched in front of the French doors that lead out to our back yard, every inch of their poise and posture proclaiming, *I was born to kill birds and bunnies, and that's just what I'm going to do*—tickles me to no end.

Who's mommy's little hunter? I croon fondly. *Who's my fuzzy-wuzzy wizzle attack kitty?*

I should probably add here that my cats are strictly indoor-only and have never even come close to killing a bird or a bunny—or anything else furry, winged, or crawling, with the exception of the occasional palmetto bug or housefly unfortunate enough to make it inside. The most my cats can do is watch with quivering haunches and full-black murder eyes from behind reinforced glass.

And while I would be absolutely horrified, were I to actually witness my beloved felines dispatching one of those fledgling robins I've become so emotionally invested in, seeing my cats tremble with the desire—and very clear intent—to do so inevitably leaves me shaking my head lovingly while murmuring an affectionate, *Awwwwwwwww!* under my breath.

What can I say? I tend to love things for being what they are. I love the birds for flying and building their nests, the squirrels for scampering after nuts and eating breadcrumbs so daintily with their tiny paws, the opossum mama for carrying her wee babes in a row on her back...

And I love my own sweet little house panthers, who are nearly bursting with their insatiable desire to horribly, horribly murder each and every last one of them.

PAWSOME!

You sit in one position as long as humanly possible, just because your cat is comfy

It's a scorching midsummer day and your air conditioner is broken. With each second that goes by, your legs are getting sweatier and sweatier beneath their burden of snoozing cat-flesh—not to mention more filled with pins and needles than a dressmaker's etui. (Crossword-ese for "pretty box that holds sewing stuff.")

Any rational person would have long-since shoved the sleepy kitty from their lap and stretched out their legs to restore blood circulation and air flow. Not you, though. You grit your teeth, mop your brow, declare that your only regret is having but one lap to dedicate to feline-kind, and then give that adorably fuzzy heat-bag on your legs an additional scritch under the chin for good measure.

Superman may be made of steel, but *you* are made of **PAWSOME**!

You talk to your cats like they can understand you

S ure, know-nothing strangers may find the running conversation you have with your cats deeply odd. After all, they'll point out oh-so-smugly, it's not like your cats understand what you're saying. And what's even the point of talking to someone who can't talk back to you?

Well, I'm not so sure that our cats can't understand what we're saying. (My own cats, for example, have the uncanny ability to know when my husband and I are discussing dinner plans or vet appointments). And anyone who's spent enough time around cats—with their colorful range of meows, mews, chirps, chitters, and purrs—knows that cats have a complete and *very* expressive language all their own.

But even if none of that were true, the bottom line is that your cats can certainly tell *when* you're saying something to them, even if they have no idea *what* you're saying. And, judging by the spirited mews and purrs with which they greet the sound of your voice, just being included in the conversation makes a cat feel good.

And isn't making somebody else feel good one of the very best reasons for doing anything at all?

Not that you need *me* to tell you that. Living with cats has already made you the kind of person who loves doing all the little things that make someone else happy—even if ignorant onlookers are incapable of seeing the value in it.

PAWSOME!

You refrain from rubbing your cat's belly

If you're a cat lover (and, honestly, why wouldn't you be?), then you probably find kitty bellies well-nigh irresistible.

My own cat Fanny has a habit of rolling around seductively on her back, flashing her fuzzy underside until the cuteness of it is more than mortal flesh can bear...and then quickly contracting into a veritable Venus flytrap—claws and teeth snapping shut around my fingers—the instant they make contact with her tummy.

Cats, as a general rule, prefer not to have their bellies rubbed—a point they are more than willing to drive home with the kind of emphasis that often leaves ailurophiles reaching for the band-aids and rubbing alcohol.

The truly maddening thing is that cats are apt to roll over and display those fluffy, scrumptious, maddeningly rub-able undercarriages when they're at their most relaxed and trusting—in short, when your cat is about as adorable as the laws of physics will allow any living creature to be. The impulse to sink your fingers into that delectable fluff can be a sorer temptation than a warm brownie sundae after a month of dieting.

Nevertheless, knowing as you well do how irritating most moggies find it to have their bellies rubbed—and how giving cats such utterly enticing bellies, and then programming them to hate having those bellies even *touched*, is surely evidence that God enjoys practical jokes—you hold back. Your hands remain firmly in your pockets while the tantalizing little succubus who shares your home wriggles around on his back, blissfully unaware (or, perhaps, all *too* aware) of the agony he's inflicting on you.

You hold back because you have willpower. Because you respect the rights of this independent creature you live with and because, no matter how tempted you may be, you don't want to undermine his sense of security or autonomy by imposing your will on his own.

In other words: Because you're **PAWSOME**!

But sometimes you rub your cat's belly!

O f course, every so often you'll run across the unusual cat who actually *likes* having his tummy rubbed. My own Clayton is just such a cat—one who'll jump into my lap, promptly flip onto his back, and all but *demand* that I make with the belly rubs, posthaste.

 If you have a tummy-rub-loving cat, then you know what it's like to sit there in one spot, scritching away, as the evening news gives way to primetime and eventually melts into the late-night talk shows. Your hand grows as numb as your legs beneath the weight of your cat, while you forgo food, sleep, or even a slightly more comfortable sitting position.

All because your cat is purring so contentedly under your ministrations that you couldn't *possibly* bear to disturb him.

And also because you're **PAWSOME!**

You're the only one who understands what your cat is "saying"

C ats tend to develop their "vocabularies" around their own specific and unique concerns. My tripod cat Clayton has his "Throw my fetching toy!" meow. My cat Scarlett—a creature of rather fastidious habits—had a cry that meant "My litter box is not adequately clean!" And my blind cat, Homer—who had neither faith in, nor knowledge of, the many visual cues a cat can offer—had a rich and subtle vocabulary capable of conveying everything from, "Pay attention to me!" to "I want tuna, not turkey!" to "You're sleeping WAY too late!" (This last injunction—usually offered in the predawn darkness that a blind cat could perhaps be forgiven for not noticing—was always particularly mortifying.)

The thing is, though, it's not like there's any *universal* cat language that you, as a cat lover, could learn once and for all and then apply to every subsequent feline who pads through your life. Learning your specific cat's particular whims, fancies, and preferences takes real effort and patience—along with the commitment to someone else's peace of mind that only arises in the closest and most meaningful of relationships.

Although the way your cat would probably express it would be more like, "My human is *sooooooo* easy to train! That's why he's **PAWSOME!**"

You speak to your cats in that special voice that's just for them

Every "cat person" has a "cat voice." That silly-but-affectionate voice you only use when speaking directly to your cat—preferably when nobody else is around to hear it.

No two cat voices sound exactly alike. Your own might be high and squeaky or low and rumbly, or it might flow from between your lips with a spirited, sing-song cadence. Maybe you say perfectly coherent (if not exactly intelligent) things in your cat voice, like: "Who wants nom-noms? Do *you*? Do *you* want nom-noms?" Or perhaps you go full-unintelligible-babble with something like, "Whodaitsybitsyfuzzywizzlenomnomkitty???"

And maybe your cat, upon hearing this loveable nonsense, glows with the knowledge that she's being singled out as special. Maybe she even "talks" back to you with those specific mews or meows that you—and only you—are capable of interpreting correctly.

Maybe she simply rolls her eyes. Or whatever the feline equivalent of eye rolling is.

However it goes down, the one constant is that, for just that moment, your cat knows to a certainty that she's the sole focus of your attention—that you're not speaking to anybody else in the whole wide world except her.

And *you* get the satisfaction of knowing that you've made your beloved kitty feel just a little bit more beloved.

PAWSOME!

Sometimes you sit on the floor with your cat

C ats spend so much time on the floor—snoozing, scampering, rolling around on their backs in a puddle of sunlight—that it can be easy to forget how much time we humans *don't* spend on the floor.

Sure, we *walk* on the floor. But lying on the floor—without so much as a yoga mat for a cushion—is the pits. Sleeping on the floor is brutal torture. Even sitting on the floor isn't all that much fun, particularly as you get older and getting back up *off* the floor becomes a real challenge.

Maybe that's why your cat is so darn tickled on those occasions when you throw caution and comfort to the wind and hunker down on the tiles—or possibly even lie down and stretch out full length—just so your cat can have the joy of climbing, perching, burrowing, and snuggling all over you from his preferred floor-bound vantage point rather than on a chair, sofa, or bed like he's used to doing.

Those times when you actually join your kitty at floor level are a full-fledged special occasion. It's an instant *paw*ty, and it's pretty **PAWSOME!**

You brush your cats to get rid of dry skin and old fur

It keeps their fur from getting matted. It improves their circulation. And it feels soooooooooooo good...
PAWSOME!

Doody-butt!!!

Maybe you call it something different in your house.

Maybe you don't have a name for it at all. Maybe you've never heard yourself, of a quiet Sunday morning, hollering to your husband who's downstairs making coffee, "Bring up some toilet paper! We've got a Category 5 doody-butt emergency!"

I'm referring, of course, to the unpleasant but well-nigh inevitable eventuality of having your cat step into the litterbox to do his business, then exit said litterbox having sadly failed to leave *everything* behind.

Sometimes your cat remains blissfully unaware of the problem. Sometimes he's *entirely* aware, scooting his hind-quarters frantically across white rugs and fresh bedsheets and assorted pieces of tough-to-clean furniture—or perhaps even (as my Clayton does) attempting to outrun the sticky stowaway, which is about as effective as trying to treat a headache with leeches.

Regardless, dollars to donuts your cat will both desperately need your help to resolve the matter, and also at the same time adamantly refuse to accept any help from you whatsoever.

Many's the time I've found myself, roll of toilet paper clutched in my hand, racing around the house after a fleeing cat—knowing that my eventual reward, when I finally do catch her, will be the joy of using said toilet paper to pull poop from her *tuchus* fur like I was trying to get peanut butter out of a shag rug.

Unpleasant as it is, however, when push comes to shove (comes to poop), you roll up our sleeves and get in there to handle the sticky situation like the champ you are.

Being a cat-parent ain't always glamorous, but that's the motherflipping job.

PAWSOME!

You score weed for your cat

You've never broken the law in your entire life.

Never so much as claimed an even slightly questionable tax deduction. Never sped through an "orange" traffic light. Never carved your sweetheart's name into a tree at the park or taken a chewed-up wad of gum out of your mouth and stuck it the underside of a desk.

When it comes to walking the straight-and-narrow, you could teach a Master Class.

Which is what makes it all the more surprising to onlookers (although not, I can assure you, to your fellow cat lovers) when you oh-so-casually walk in with an ounce of that wacky feline weed *nepeta cataria* (otherwise known as garden-variety catnip), sprinkle some around the floor, and watch as your cat proceeds to get as high as a Georgia pine.

PAWSOME!

You remember to turn off the flash so your cat doesn't get "laser eyes" in photos

O kay, so maybe you don't *always* remember to do this. And maybe your cat doesn't actually care about looking like she has "laser eyes" in photos. Maybe, if she could be made to understand what laser eyes were, she'd even think it was kinda cool. *It looks like my eyes are shooting lasers!* she'd say. *Badass!*

But *you* know that laser eyes tend to look doofy in a finished photo—not so much like your cat is a lethal warrior goddess, but more like she got caught unawares when you pointed the camera at her face, which makes her just as apt to have one of those unprepared, unflattering, open-mouthed, *derp* expressions that make the rest of us dread seeing candid photos of ourselves even more than we dread doing our taxes every year. (And I'm a freelancer, so that's, like, a *lot* of dread!)

The point is that you're the kind of person who looks out for others even when they're not looking out for themselves. And the way you do your level best to make sure your kitty looks just as adorable in every picture you snap of her as she does in the furry flesh is merely one more example of just how **PAWSOME** you are!

You let your cat have all the pillows

When you walk into your bedroom and see your cat asleep on the bed, sprawled out strategically so that some part of her body—one outstretched paw, perhaps, or the very tip of her tail—is at least slightly touching each and every pillow on the bed, do you shove her out of the way so that you can lie down yourself?

Or do you say *Awwwwwwwwww* and leave kitty to her luxurious slumber?

Yeah...that's what I thought. Ya big softy!

PAWSOME!

You let your cat sleep on clean clothes fresh from the dryer

It can never be too hot for my cats—particularly Fanny, who's never happier than in the oppressive summertime heat of the sundrenched primary bedroom on the very top floor of our very old house (full of Victorian-era charm, but sadly *sans* central AC). Fanny likes to sprawl out full-length in the sweltering bedroom while snoozing contentedly in the biggest sun puddle she can find, soaking up the intense warmth until her coal-black fur feels like actual hot coals.

Unfortunately for Fanny, there are too many months in the year when the thermometer barely rises above freezing here in the Northeast—months when the angle of the sun is such that even the occasional sun puddle becomes a rare treat rather than a daily occurrence.

But on the plus side for Fanny—and for all those other heat-worshipping cats like her—there's always once-a-week laundry to look forward to, and the inevitable bag, basket, or pile of clean clothing fresh out of the dryer. Clothing that's still warm to the touch and thus an absolutely *purr*-fect spot for a not-so-quick catnap.

Of course, one of the main goals that a cat lover's weekly washing has to accomplish is the removal of cat fur from all the shirts, sheets, pants, towels, and so on where it tends to accumulate. Simple logic would therefore seem to dictate that allowing a cat to immediately lie all over that freshly de-furred clothing might be just a tad self-defeating.

But allow me to counter that seemingly flawless reasoning by asking a simple question: Is there anything more adorable on the whole face of the earth than the sight of a sweetly sleeping cat curled up smack-dab in the middle of a huge mound of clothing? And isn't it kind of worth doing all the work of sorting and cleaning and drying your clothes, just for this deeply gratifying sight?

After all, there's always the prospect of next week's laundry—and newly fur-free clothes—ahead of you. And, as a wise internet meme has pointed out, rich people may have designer labels on their clothing, but *happy* people have cat fur on theirs.

PAWSOME!

You bring Da Bird to life

A bunch of feathers glued to the end of a string that's glued to the end of a stick might not sound like an invention whose importance equals that of moving pictures, say, or the polio vaccine.

But as far as your cat is concerned, it's a concoction of sheer wizardry—and *you* are the only being advanced enough to bring it to magical life!

You make it dance and spin. You make it fly high in the air and then dip perilously close to crashing on the ground before it rebounds to hang just above your kitty's nose, tantalizing her nearly to the point of madness. In a good way.

It's just about her favorite game, aside from Biting Toes Under The Covers and Pushing Things Off The Table—except that in *this* game nothing gets bruised, cracked, or otherwise damaged, aside from maybe a cluster of feathers that was designed for that exact purpose.

And it's all thanks to *you*—your home's Imagineer in Chief. **PAWSOME!**

You probably saved your cat's life when you adopted him

E very year in the U.S. alone, some six-point-three million companion animals end up in shelters.

Roughly half of those companion animals are cats. About one-third of those cats will eventually be euthanized. And that's not even counting the number of stray cats who would benefit enormously from living in loving homes—who, in many cases, have been abandoned by humans who once cared for them but then, one day, simply tossed them out—and who languish outside of the shelter system, but are no less desperate for it.

Which is why it's no exaggeration to say that you almost certainly saved your cat's life when you adopted him.

But even if you adopted your cat from a no-kill shelter—someplace that would have guaranteed your kitty a caring lifelong home even if you'd never swooped in to save the day—you've nevertheless still saved a life. By adopting one cat, you've opened up a much-needed space in that no-kill shelter for another cat to be saved.

I realize I'm leaving out cat-parents who may have obtained their beloved feline friends from a breeder. Although my own inclinations tend toward #adoptdontshop, I realize that ethical breeders play an important role in the cat-loving community. Love is love, after all, no matter how it ends up coming into our lives.

Still, the sheer number of rescue-cat adopters who swear up and down that "I didn't save her, *she* saved *me*!" should give you pause—and hopefully lead you to at least consider the possibility of adopting a rescue cat the next time around.

The life you save may be your own.

PAWSOME!

You let your cat follow you into the bathroom

I've heard some ailurophiles say they have a closer and more intimate relationship with their cat than with their significant other.

If I'm being totally honest, I have to admit that—close as my husband and I are—there are any number of intimate things that my cats, and *only* my cats, will ever see me do. Some are of the goofy, dancing-around-the-house-in-your-underwear variety that you can't quite bring yourself to let anybody see. But most take place in that most private of private spaces, the *sanctum sanctorum* of every household.

I refer, of course, to the bathroom.

There are things I do in the bathroom that my husband has never seen and will never see (if there's any god at all). It's not that I worry my husband would love me less if he happened to see me sitting on the toilet or shaving my armpits. (Although seeing me do both simultaneously might take some of the bloom off the rose.)

It's just that I'd rather engage in these activities without any kind of an audience *at all*. And for that reason it took me a minute to adjust to having my cats with me in the bathroom—and, furthermore, to having a cat with me in the bathroom *at all times*, no matter what I happened to be doing.

My Vashti—the second cat I ever adopted—used to sit at my feet and watch with rapt attention as I applied makeup, and her successor, my current cat Fanny, enjoys doing so to this day. My clingy Clayton, unusually for a cat, never needs or wants any time alone, and seems to resent even the implication that I might desire five cat-free minutes in my day. In his old age, my cat Homer used to curl up atop the clothes hamper while I showered, and snooze peacefully in the warmth of the steam. *Like an old man taking a shvitz,* I would tell my husband.

Perhaps you also have an instinctive desire for strict bathroom privacy. But perhaps you, like me, find yourself wondering, *Is there really any good reason to lock my cats out? Especially when it seems to make them so happy to be in here?*

And that, as always, is the best and final argument.

How could you bring yourself to deny your cat those small moments of joy she appears to experience when sitting at your feet, looking up at you intently as you masque your face, or curl your eyelashes, or clasp that one errant chin hair firmly betwixt your tweezers and give it a good yank?

And it's not like there's anybody else who could sit there watching you do these things and *still* maintain a glow in their eyes that clearly says, *You're the most fascinating creature on the face of the earth!*

PAWSOME!

You don't stare at your cats, even when they stare at you

I f cats could talk, this would be a classic, "Do as I say, not as I do," situation.

Actually, cats *do* kind of talk to us—with their varied meows, for example (indicating everything from "feed me now" to "that dog outside is scaring me!"), or with their posture and how they hold their tails.

And a cat who's staring straight at you is definitely trying to communicate something. Generally speaking, if your cat is staring at you, it should be interpreted as a sign of affection—especially if it's accompanied by a few slow blinks.

On the other hand, you should DEFINITELY not stare back at your cat! An unwavering, unblinking stare will be construed as a sign of aggression and will most likely get her literal and figurative back up.

In short, it's a bad idea to stare at your cat. But when your cat stares at *you*, on the other hand...well that's

PAWSOME!

You protect your cat through thick and thin from everything scary in the world...

I t's no exaggeration to say that—were it necessary to do so—you would take a bullet for your cat.

Fortunately, everyday life rarely presents situations of such dramatic intensity. Most of what you'll be "protecting" your cat from will be garden variety—the startling loudness of a car backfiring outside; the shifty-looking dog whose human walks him by your window every morning; the *Mad Men* opening-credits sequence, which some cats find inexplicably terrifying. (My Clayton runs in abject terror when the "falling man" makes his first appearance, and it takes him a good ten minutes to recover his equanimity).

Whether it's a veterinarian's needle or a friend's ill-behaved child or an actual lunatic shooter, there's nothing in this world so fierce, frightening, or downright petrifying that you wouldn't stand between *it* and your cat.

You may not be one of those people who can bench press their own body weight. Nevertheless, when it comes to defending your cat, you're strong and immovable as the Great Wall of China.

PAWSOME!

...But you still make your cat feel like a fierce, brave hunter!

[To be read in an only slightly patronizing baby voice:]
Who's mommy's brave little hunter? Yes you are! YES YOU ARE!
PAWSOME!

You give your cats their favorite human foods

S haring a meal with others is one of the oldest and most important rituals of communal bonding in human history. The same is true of human-*feline* history.

Anthropologists say that cats first started hanging around humans once we began farming, because of the plentiful rodents our storehouses of food would regularly attract.

Seeing how my cats react whenever I unwrap a package of deli cheese, however, I'm guessing that the food itself was also a pretty big draw.

Fast-forward a few millennia to your own present-day household, and ask yourself what your cat would do without you and your ability to open cans of tuna, dismantle a turkey sandwich, or pull bits of cooked chicken from the bone—and then distribute this bounty to your waiting (and famished) feline friend?

My cats have assured me in no uncertain terms that they would starve—*starve*, I tell you!—if not for the near-constant stream of morsels from my own plate, bowl, or to-go container directed their way.

Chances are your cats have made you similar assurances of encroaching famine, and the necessity of fending it off with samples of your own meals.

And, also, you probably just have a lot of fun spoiling your kitties rotten.

PAWSOME!

You turn on the bathroom faucet so your cat can play in the water

I once spent seventy-five dollars on a Hammacher Schlemmer cat fountain because one of my cats was so very, very enraptured by running water—whether it came out of the kitchen sink or the bathtub faucet—that I figured I'd make us both happy (her directly, me vicariously) by giving her the gift of constant running water, whenever she wanted it.

Stop me if you already know where this story is going.

I guess they wouldn't make cat fountains if there weren't cats out there who actually liked them. Sadly for me, however, not one of my five ever has—not even the ones who were really into running water and more or less demanded it of me, repeatedly, throughout the course of the day.

Science will tell you that cats find running water to be more "natural" and hygienic, which is why they're so fascinated by it. And while that may very well be true, I have no doubt that the fun of getting their human to jump up so obligingly whenever a little bathtub playtime is requested is a big part of the attraction (for *my* cats, anyway).

Vexing as it often was to have a cat demanding I turn on the faucet for her while I was in the middle of trying to finish a tricky paragraph ahead of a writing deadline, or struggling into a too-tight pair of jeans, or getting comfortable on the couch with my husband, I suppose I can understand why the appeal of running water might lessen when it suddenly becomes available *all the time*. Scarcity is the secret sauce that adds flavor to so many of the things we love most, like the holiday meals that only come once a year, or the appearance of the ice cream truck that only cruises your block once or twice a week.

And while I didn't necessarily love having to stop whatever I was doing whenever the whim struck my faucet-loving cat, her insistence that it be the faucet—and not something she could access herself whenever she wanted—made me appreciate those scarce and fleeting pleasures in my own life that much more.

PAWSOME!

You brush your cat's teeth

I've been a cat guardian for more than twenty-five years now—and, for the past decade or so, a very public one who spends the majority of her days engaging with other cat-parents online and in person—so I thought I'd heard pretty much everything on the subject of cat care.

You can imagine my shock, therefore, when I read an article in the *Atlantic* a couple of months ago about people who brush their cats' teeth at home.

Let me say that again: There are people out there who take a toothbrush and toothpaste, load a squirt of said toothpaste onto the toothbrush, force brush and paste into their unwilling cats' clenched mouths, and *brush their cats' teeth for them.*

(!!!)

Not only is home-cat-tooth-brushing apparently a bona fide *thing*, by the way, but it's a thing that a small subset of intrepid cat guardians do *several times a week!*

Did you know about this?!!?

I'm going to guess that the vast majority of cat custodians do *not* brush their cats' teeth at home on the regular (although I do dispense a daily dose of Dental Greenies, for whatever that's worth)—and I'm going to guess further that *you*, dear reader, probably don't either.

But even if you, like me, sensibly leave your cats' dental care to trained professionals, you've undoubtedly done all kinds of other invasive and unpleasant things—things that your cats hated at the time, and possibly hated you for doing—for the sake of safeguarding their health and wellbeing. If the phrase "kitty burrito" (a method of wrapping a cat in a towel or blanket so as to trim her claws, force pills down her throat, inject a needle into the back of her neck, et cetera) strikes a resonant chord with you, then you know what I'm talking about.

Cats are indisputably adorable, and they fill our hearts and our homes with joy, laughter, and considerable entertainment. But living with a cat isn't *all* sunshine and roses. No matter how good the good times are, eventually things will get real—and you'll find yourself filling the role of live-in nurse, dealing with the up-close-and-personal realities of a fragile and aging feline body that you're responsible for keeping alive and healthy for as long as that's possible.

It's a tough job, and it's an often thankless one. (Your cat certainly isn't going to thank you!) There's no national "Cat Parents' Day." Hallmark doesn't make a card that says, *Thanks for taking such great care of your cats!* Nobody will ever hand you a trophy for doing it, or give you the key to the city, or throw you a parade.

But you weren't doing it for any of those things, anyway.
PAWSOME!

You take care of your cat when she's sick

I t's a given that no home can be truly happy if there aren't any cats in it. But that doesn't mean living with a cat is all sunshine and roses.

Just like the rest of us, cats get sick sometimes. Even the healthiest kitty is apt to come down with the occasional cold or tummy bug, or twist her leg while jumping from a high-up shelf. And should you be lucky enough to avoid all the minor scrapes and skirmishes, the inevitability of old age—with its attendant illnesses and indignities—is still awaiting your cat down the road.

Like most longtime cat guardians, I've found myself having to treat wounds, change bandages, gently wash the fur of a kitty so ill that she got sick all over herself, administer pills and shots, and occasionally force-feed a cat with baby food and water mixed in a syringe. (A cat with a head cold who can't smell her food is apt to refuse to eat it, which is not at all the same thing as saying that a cat with a head cold *doesn't need* to eat.)

That my cats greeted these efforts on my part—however tenderly offered—with extreme resistance will come as a surprise to exactly no one.

You would think that after years and years of providing non-stop food and toys and cuddles, I'd have earned the teensiest bit of credibility when, for example, it comes time to give one of my cats a dose of a liquid antibiotic. Alas, you would be *very* wrong. And so I've become an expert in the "kitty burrito" method of immobilizing my cats by wrapping them up in a towel with just their head exposed—holding the struggling, wrapped-up cat to my chest with one hand while the other attempts to get the medication into her reluctant mouth and down her throat.

(One time, one of my cat's back legs wriggled free of the "kitty burrito" and left a colorful trail of welts down the front of my chest and across my upper left arm. And that's how I learned that trying to medicate a cat while wearing a scoop-necked tank top is a strictly amateur move.)

I suppose if you were a certain kind of fair-weather friend, you'd enjoy the good times when they come—all the purrs and snuggles and delightful games of "chase the toy mouse"—while leaving your felines to fend for themselves when those good times turn decidedly less fun.

But you made a commitment to your cat the day you brought him into your life—a commitment to stand by his side and take care of him in sickness and health, no matter what. You did so knowing that love isn't always pretty and can sometimes be downright unpleasant.

But you also knew that taking the good with the bad is precisely what real love is all about.

Besides, you were never the type to bail when the going gets tough, anyway.

PAWSOME!

You take your cat to the vet, even though you both hate it

M y cat Clayton is kind of a rock star at the vet's office.

At least, you'd *think* he was a rock star based on the wildly enthusiastic greeting he receives whenever we walk in. Cries of "It's *CLAYTON!!!*" ring out from Reception in the front all the way to exam rooms in the back, as every single person we pass shoves a couple of fingers or even their whole hand through the top of Clayton's soft carrier—while Clayton himself, receiving all this adulation as no more than his fair due, purrs contentedly.

The secret of Clayton's popularity at the vet's office is really no secret at all: Clayton is one of those extraordinarily rare oddball kitties who actually likes the vet's office!

I *know!* But it's *true!*

To say that Clayton loves attention would be like saying the rest of us love oxygen. Being so utterly dependent on constant attention to get him through his days, he's not particularly partial as to where or how he gets it—not even when that attention is accompanied by intrusive fingers in his mouth, or needles in his rump, or the decidedly uncomfortable insertion of a thermometer in his backside.

The otherwise-beleaguered doctors and technicians at our vet's office are more used to cats like...well...like every other cat I've ever lived with. Cats who, upon seeing their carrier suddenly appear in the living room, will run, hide, scratch, hiss, scale impossibly tall cabinets, transform themselves into un-catchable streaks of speeding fur, and otherwise make the run-up to their vet visit among the more miserable half-hours you'll ever spend.

If you're lucky, that's the worst of it—and your cat will settle down into some more-or-less sulky form of passive resistance once you make it to the vet's office.

But every so often you have a special cat, like my Homer was. The bar-none greatest boy in the world at home, Homer was an ungodly holy terror in any medical setting. Eventually, our vet suggested in the nicest possible language that Homer probably shouldn't return to their clinic ever again—and, after assuring her that I would assume financial responsibility for any medical bills incurred by her staff as a result of Homer's visit, I was forced to concede the point.

In short: With the lovely exception of Clayton, taking my cats to the vet has been just about the most consistently harrowing thing about being a cat-mom.

My guess is that it's the same for you—that no matter how genuinely lovely and genial a person your veterinarian is, there's a small part of you that dreads any excursion to the vet's office, whether it's due to a major illness or a routine exam.

And imagine how your cat feels! Your poor kitty has no idea why you've dragged her from her safe and sunny kitty bed out into a cold cruel veterinary exam room where, in league with various medical personnel, you've inexplicably transformed from Loving Source Of Food And Comfort into Co-Conspirator With Pure Evil.

I suspect, however, that somewhere deep down, your cat knows that even this outrage—like just about everything else you do—reflects how very deep your love for her runs. That even though seeing how utterly miserable she is makes you more miserable than words could ever express, you'd suffer this and worse a thousand times over, if it means making sure your beloved feline companion stays healthy and happy for years and years to come.

PAWSOME!

You touch your nose to your cat's nose

Humans greet other humans with handshakes. Cats greet other cats—especially cats they already know—by touching noses. And while the minor exchange of scents that occurs between cats when they touch noses isn't really *your* thing, you understand how much this friendly little gesture means to your kitty.

So you touch your nose to her nose. And she touches her nose to yours. And the whole thing is sooooooooooooo sweet that it's more than just adorable.

It's **PAWSOME!**

You debase yourself for your cats' amusement

M y husband used to think I was sharp as a tack. My keen intellect was one of the things that first drew him to me, he always said. That and a general air of cosmopolitan sophistication.

Then I moved into his apartment with my three cats. It was no more than a day or two into our cohabitation when my husband (then-boyfriend) heard me, in a goofy falsetto, query of my cat Homer, "Was dose nom-noms so nummy? Was dey so nummy in yo wizzle tummy?"

It's probably not an exaggeration to say that, in the eighteen years since, his opinion of my intellect hasn't entirely recovered.

What can I say? A fear of looking foolish isn't really one of my biggest fears. It comes well behind, for example, a fear of finding hairs on my chin (this has happened three times since I turned fifty), or a spider in my bed, or pretty much anything that would require me to spend some significant amount of time in any kind of natural setting that wasn't a beach.

And while I'd generally prefer *not* to look foolish in front of others, the things that tickle my cats' fancy tend to take precedence. Besides, as I've painstakingly explained to my husband more times than I can count, if I *don't* speak to my cats in that voice, how will they know I'm talking to them and not somebody else?

Who among us hasn't found themselves wriggling around on their belly so as to be at cat's-eye level when playing a game of Swipe The Toy Mouse In My Hand? Or babbling incoherently in their special talking-to-my-cat voice?

And, sure, I sometimes find myself intimidated by those frighteningly put-together women I see on TV or roaming the streets of Manhattan. Women in four-figure suits with the kind of straight shiny hair that *somebody* obviously spent hours blowing out for them, and who look as if phrases like *nom noms* and *fuzzy wuzzy* would never in a million years cross their immaculately made-up lips.

But then I reflect that those women have probably never known the joys of donning a plastic hula skirt still hanging around your closet from some decades-old Halloween party, and swishing it around like a person in the throes of some sort of fit, just for the sheer fun of watching your cat chase after you while swiping furiously at the fringe.

PAWSOME!

You build your schedule around your cat's schedule

D og owners are forever being valorized for their high-intensity commitment to their furry pals—blowing off after-work outings so they can rush home and walk their dogs; taking their dogs for walks even during typhoons and blizzards; and devoting hours and hours to hanging out at dog parks solely for their dogs' benefit.

This very public sacrifice of scarce personal time at the altar of dog worship is one reason, I think, why dog owners are perceived as being more "social" and "well adjusted" than cat people—not only because all that time spent watching dogs socialize at dog parks seems to imply lots of human interaction, as well (although mostly what I see at the dog park is people sitting on benches and checking their cell phones, while pointedly ignoring their fellow dog owners), but also because the conspicuous sacrifice of one's precious time for the sake of the greater good is the very glue that holds society together.

Antisocial cat people, on the other hand (or so the general perception goes), have cats instead of dogs because they selfishly wanted a companion animal who wouldn't impose on their free time.

The thing with cats and their guardians is that cats spend the majority of their time indoors, far from public view. There's nothing even a little bit performative about all that time you spend doing things with and for your cats, because nobody's ever around to see any of it. Even in the case of the cats whose humans walk them outdoors on leashes, they're not taking those cats to "cat parks" or following them around with little poop bags, or leaving them tied to a nearby chair at some outdoor café while their human enjoys brunch with friends.

It's this very lack of visibility that makes it seem as though dog owners are endlessly self-sacrificing, while cat owners...not so much.

What almost nobody outside your innermost circle is ever likely to see is how much of your schedule is built around your cat's schedule. Cats are creatures of habit, after all, and, to the greatest extent possible, cats like doing the same things at the exact same times every day.

Which is why you get up early even on your days off to feed your cat at the time he's used to. It's why you let your cat, who's accustomed to being in bed with you from precisely 11:00 p. m. until 7:00 a.m. every night, sprawl all over you even when a bout of insomnia would probably pass more quickly if you had the bed to yourself. It's why you're infinitely more discerning about whom you allow into the inner sanctum of your life and your home—the one and only place in the whole world where your cat feels entirely comfortable and secure—than the caretakers of an easygoing dog are required to be.

Cat guardians don't get as much glory for their constancy because it tends to manifest itself in that same place where our innermost hearts always live: within the privacy of our very own homes.

PAWSOME!

Sometimes you break down and smell your cat's butt

I mean, it would be kinda hard *not* to, given how frequently it seems to end up pressed right against your face...
At least your cat keeps it pretty clean, right???
PAWSOME!

You always give your cat a lap to sit on

Everybody remembers *The Giving Tree*, Shel Silverstein's parable about a selfless apple tree who loved a little boy and gave him all of herself—her apples for him to eat, her branches for him to climb (and later to build a house with), her leaves to shade his head, and her trunk for him to carve into a boat. Eventually the tree was nothing more than a stump—but still she had one final thing to offer up: a place for the boy, now an elderly man, to sit and rest.

To my fellow selfless cat lovers out there, I say: We are all that Giving Tree.

Of course, not every cat actually wants to sit on us or snuggle into our laps. For sixteen years, I had the exclusive love of a "surly girl" named Scarlett, who never craved much in the way of physical affection beyond a desire to sprawl behind me on the back of the couch and rest a single paw on my shoulder while she slept. My cat Homer, on the other hand, demanded *lots* of physical contact—although what he primarily wanted was to lean against my leg rather than lie on it. My cat Vashti eschewed laps and legs entirely in favor of lying on the chests of the humans she especially liked.

These days I'm owned by two true-blue lap cats, and rare are the times when neither my husband nor I have a cat sprawled across our legs. In fact, just finding a handful of lap-cat-free moments over the course of the day—to use the restroom, perhaps, or to engage in a bit of husband/wife alone time—can be a job of work, one inevitably accompanied by a series of bitterly drawn-out feline complaints that could only be translated as: *But whyyyyyyyyyyyyyyyyyyyyy?!?!?*

The point, however, isn't whether your cat sleeps on your literal lap. The point is that, dollars to donuts, whatever it is your cat wants from you, you offer it up gladly—even if what you have to offer is nothing more than a warm place for her to lay her weary kitty head.

The Giving Tree's got nothing on you.

PAWSOME!

You fish your cat's toys out from under the couch and refrigerator

Every so often, I'll notice that the floors of my home—normally covered in a thin layer of crinkle balls, rattling felt mice, catnip sachets, and wadded up takeout receipts—seem suspiciously clean. I'll make it all the way from the staircase through the living room and into the kitchen without having to sidestep so much as a single plastic spring. *That's odd,* I'll think. *I haven't done any housecleaning since [INSERT DATE AT LEAST TWO MONTHS PREVIOUS].*

While I loathe dirt and generally try to stay on top of the dust situation due to allergies, I'm not exactly a neat freak—and I've been more than happy over the years to relinquish the floors of my home to the cats. They, in turn, have converted our throw rugs into scratch pads, our standing knick-knacks into...well...into more scratch pads, and our floorboards and tiles themselves into a kind of ad-hoc toybox.

So when I encounter a tidy floor—knowing, as I do, that it certainly has nothing to do with my own endeavors—it can mean only one thing: All the cat toys in the house have migrated to one of two Toy Graveyards.

I refer, of course, to the space under the sofa and the crevice beneath the refrigerator.

The rule that any and all cat toys will eventually end up under some large piece of furniture —including items that are only incidentally "cat toys," like used tin-foil balls or yarn-tasseled bookmarks—is as immutable as Newton's laws of motion. Given the endless batting-around of said toys that the typical cat engages in, simple physics demands that, eventually, an overly enthusiastic swipe will direct the item in question to the irresistible gravitational pull of the black hole under the couch or below the fridge.

Some of this is deliberate, cats being pretty much addicted to hiding things and then "finding" them a few seconds or even a few days later. In our house, hiding a small plastic mouse beneath the living-room area rug on Tuesday, where it can be rediscovered on Friday, is a little gift that Past Clayton likes to leave for Future Clayton—or, occasionally, for Present Mom, who's apt to stumble witlessly into the sharp corner of an end table upon accidentally tripping over the unexpected lump in the rug.

The only trouble, of course, is that even the best-laid plans of mice and men (and cats) are apt to go awry. Inevitably, your cat will be so successful at "hiding" some favored toy—or so *un*successful at keeping it in play—that it will be up to you to lie flat down on your belly with your cheek welded to the floor, clutching a broom or unbent coat hanger or maybe even an actual fishing pole, while you grope around in the hopes of unearthing Mopsy's and Mittens' favorite playthings.

It's a dirty job—especially in my house, where chances are nobody's swept under the sofa or refrigerator since the *last* time we had to fish out all the cat toys—but it's one you do without complaining, simply because you're an amazing human who loves your cat.

PAWSOME!

You change the channel when there's something scary on TV

P erhaps you live with what I'll call a "noise-sensitive" cat.

Maybe you've gotten used to opening new trash bags veeeeeeeeerrrrry slooooooooooowly rather than with a decisive *snap!* Maybe you take your shoes off the moment you enter the house—not for the sake of hygiene, but because the sound of heels clicking briskly across hardwood floors leaves your cat convinced the Apocalypse has arrived. Maybe every time you open a stepladder with a loud *CLANG!* is a newly traumatic event for your cat, one that requires you to stop whatever you're doing and comfort him before you can resume the task at hand.

If this describes you and your cat, chances are you gave up watching jump-scare movies in your house a long time ago. The same holds true for movies with lots of loud shooting sequences, including just about anything in the explosive Marvel or *Star Wars* canons. My husband and I have even learned to hit the "skip intro" button ASAP when watching old *Mad Men* reruns, because something about the combination of the opening-credits music and the silhouetted "falling man" scares our poor Clayton nearly out of his wits.

That last example just goes to prove that you can never be entirely sure ahead of time what's going to set a sensitive kitty off. Sometimes the most innocuous thing onscreen will send a startled Bootsie skittering for cover, while you're left to suss out what it was, exactly, about the bucolic British countryside in that episode of *Father Brown Murder Mysteries* that scared the bejesus out of your poor puss.

Not that it really matters—because, in the end, you do what needs to be done: You put your own viewing pleasure on pause, decide to wait until you're alone later on to find out whodunit, and open up that peaceful "TV For Cats" streaming app you downloaded onto your Fire Cube for just such an occasion.

Seriously, though...*whodunit???*

PAWSOME!

You don't get offended when your cat starts vigorously cleaning himself the second you stop petting him

A s with so many mysterious feline behaviors, the question, "Why does my cat vigorously groom himself the second I stop petting him?" has any number of theoretical answers.

It might be because your cat is itchy or sensitive in that one spot you were just petting. Or perhaps because he's replicating the kind of grooming behavior he would have experienced with his biological mom (i.e. where she teaches her kittens to groom by grooming them with her tongue and then having them groom themselves). Sometimes it may be indicative of an underlying problem, like chronically dry skin or an over-sensitivity to touch known as hyperesthesia syndrome, which can make petting an uncomfortable or even painful experience for your kitty.

But, in most cases, the answer's a pretty simple one: Cats just like grooming themselves.

Like, they really, *really* like grooming themselves—so much so that anywhere from 30% to 50% of their waking hours are spent on grooming. (A statistic that would have impressed even the vainest of my college sorority sisters.)

Cats are also pretty fastidious when it comes to things like cleanliness and odor, and no matter how much your cat might enjoy smelling your scent (you *are* her favorite person, after all!), she doesn't necessarily want to smell you all over herself.

This distinction sounds reasonable enough, but it can still feel kind of…well…maybe a little insulting when your cat deploys her raspy tongue to the patch of fur you were just petting, and cleans with the kind of intensity you probably wouldn't exhibit in your own personal grooming unless you'd just taken an accidental tumble into a septic tank.

You might even find yourself inclined to sniff under your arms and wonder aloud—à la Duckie in *Pretty in Pink*—"Do I *offend*?"

But it's hard to feel *too* offended when every moment your cat spends grooming is an opportunity for you to appreciate the adorable perfection of her pink and oh-so-raspy tongue.

PAWSOME!

You leave your cat alone when she wants to be left alone...

The way in which all cats and Greta Garbo are alike is in their frequent desire to be left *ahlone*.

Not that your cat doesn't love hanging out with you. You're her very favorite person in the whole entire world. But, still...sometimes the prospect of chilling in an empty room, gazing out of a window with nothing but your thoughts and a few wispy, trailing daydreams for company, sounds like an irresistible prospect.

There's a certain kind of person—let's call them "dog owners"—who wouldn't be able to help but take it personally if their beloved four-legged companion were to indicate a desire for a bit of solo, no-humans-allowed time.

But cat guardians are infinitely wiser. Much like our cats, we understand that a little time set aside for mental rejuvenation only makes us more attentive spouses, parents, friends, and coworkers.

And, even aside from that, solitude just feels nice sometimes. Which is why we would never want to deny that same simple pleasure to our cats.

PAWSOME!

...But you give your cat lots of attention when she wants it!

I can be walking up the stairs in my house, balancing a stack of clean laundry that goes up to my chin while simultaneously talking to my mom on the phone that's pressed between my shoulder and my ear—but if one of my cats paws at my leg, I tell mom to hold on, shuffle the laundry so it's now teetering on only one arm, and somehow manage to kneel down without pitching headlong down the staircase to find out what, exactly, my cat wants of me.

Nine times out of ten, the attention itself is what he wants.

Logically I know that there any number of things more important—or, at minimum, more immediately urgent—than whether or not one of my cats wants a scritch or a treat or even just momentary eye contact *right this second.* Cookies left in the oven even a minute too long are apt to flatten into hockey pucks. Amazon is seconds away from selling out of the $30, size 7 ½ walking shoes I love because they really do feel like walking on a cloud (which is why they sell out almost instantly). Balancing all that laundry *plus* the phone *while I'm walking up a staircase* actually requires whatever attention I can spare so as to keep from falling backwards to my death.

Between the word "death" above and this very sentence, by the way, lies an unseen 10-minute gap in my writing, during which I hoisted my three-legged Clayton onto my lap, helped him arrange himself so as to have the best view through the windows next to my desk and out to the backyard—and, of course, entirely forgot how I was going to end that last paragraph.

(I live with the persistent yet ultimately unprovable belief that an entire coherent novel could be constructed out of all the forgotten ideas, sentences, and half-grafs that will forever remain unwritten, because I stopped what I was doing to pay attention to a relentless cat.)

Magazine articles and self-help gurus are fond of telling us that we all rush around too much, that we let concerns about work and money dominate our thoughts, that we don't spend enough time being "present" when we're with our loved ones, or in our lives in general.

Maybe that's true. Still, I'm willing to bet cash money that nothing and no one is so important that it/they can't be postponed for just a minute or two, so that you can spend some mindful moments—right here, right now—giving your beloved feline all the attention she endlessly craves and oh-so-richly deserves.

PAWSOME!

You give your cat chin scritches

A nd they feel sooooooooooooo gooooooooooood...

PAWSOME!

You give your cat some tuna whenever you open a can

M aybe you've been on the receiving end of a lecture from your veterinarian about why you shouldn't feed your cats tuna. For starters, even a small portion is too high in calories for the typical cat. Eating too much of it can lead to obesity, along with all of obesity's concomitant complications (diabetes, UTIs, high blood pressure, et cetera).

And tuna is far from nutrition-ally balanced. It has too much unsaturated fat and not enough Vitamin E or any of the other antioxidants your kitty needs to stay healthy. Not to mention that tuna's high in mercury, and eating too much of it can lead to mercury poisoning.

But—with the exception of the mercury thing—couldn't the same be said about nearly any of the fun foods that *you* like to treat yourself to once in a while? Could you really make a compelling argument to your doctor along the lines of, "You don't understand, Doc. I actually *need*

to consume loaded potato skins and chocolate cheesecake on a regular basis for...um...health reasons."

By the same token, would you want to live a life utterly devoid of loaded potato skins or chocolate cheesecake?

Of course you wouldn't! And neither would your cat—for whom that giant spoonful of tuna is basically his chocolate cheesecake equivalent.

It's one thing if your veterinarian has told you there's some specific reason why your cat should never have tuna. But assuming your cat is reasonably healthy, and the dispensing of tuna is an occasional treat, then why shouldn't little Simba have some every now and then, when he clearly loves it soooooooooooooooooo much?

And isn't half the fun of opening that can of tuna for your own lunch seeing how utterly gaga your kitty gets upon hearing the whir of the can opener, knowing that in mere moments he'll be enjoying a sweet spoonful of the good stuff—dispensed by you, the amazing creature who makes all his days so fun-filled and satisfying?

PAWSOME!

You incorporate cat stuff into your decor

There are any number of feline-inspired items for the dedicated ailurophile to work into their décor if the mood strikes: cat-decorated sheets, blankets, bowls, towels, and throw pillows; cat-shaped wall clocks, lamps, bookends, and footstools; tissue dispensers and coasters that look like a cat's wazoo.

But that's not what I'm talking about here.

When I say you incorporate "cat stuff" into your décor, I mean those empty shelves on the living room wall that might look as if they're there to hold various knickknacks and bric-a-brac, but that are actually there because your cat enjoys having a high vantage point from which to survey the living room.

Or the shoe boxes that haven't held a pair of shoes for at least six months, but that do hold a fuzzy cat body for at least one hour every day.

Or that blanket still folded across the back of your couch—even though it's summer and ninety-five degrees outside, and the mere thought of a blanket makes the backs of your knees start to sweat—because no matter how hot it is outside, your cat *looooooooooves* how very warm and soft sleeping on that blanket is.

And then there's the legit cat furniture scattered about your home—climbers and scratchers and various plush beds—just because they make your kitty happy.

A visiting stranger might think you're decidedly on the "eccentric" side upon taking all this in for the first time. But who cares what judgmental strangers think? After all, the good opinion of people you barely know means infinitely less than building a home that makes it clear your cat is an essential, and much-beloved, member of your family.

PAWSOME!

You know that how you spend on your cat is more important than what you spend

Every so often, I'll see a YouTube video or online photo series about some absolute Xanadu of a cat home—a house replete with cat-sized tunnels and colorful shelves and elevated walkways all along the walls and ceilings. Maybe there's even an elaborate two-story "catio," which is a screened-in outdoor area where an indoor cat can feel like he's interacting with nature—or, at least, as much of nature as one can find in the backyards of the suburban homes where such catios are inevitably built.

But there I go, sounding kind of snide about it—when the truth is I'm so consumed with envy, I can barely see straight.

Of course I'd love to turn my home into a star-spangled maze of tactile delights for my cats. Of course there's literally nothing I see—online or IRL—that I think *might* make my cats happy without simultaneously thinking, *Should I buy this for my cats right now?* And while the dream of a catio is one that, for various logistical reasons (mainly involving the unwieldy architecture of my very old house), likely won't come to fruition anytime soon, that doesn't stop me from breaking my heart over the lack of such a luxury in my highly indulged cats' lives.

The biggest obstacle, needless to say, is money. I only have so much of it, and the lion's share is dedicated to the same wearying list of drudgeries that everyone else's is: food, shelter, health care, and responsible savings against old age and/or a possible rainy day.

And yet, I think my two cats are just about as happy as any two cats could be. I may not be able to decorate my whole house for them, but I invested in a sturdy cat tree nearly a decade ago that still looks and stands just fine, and installed it in the sunniest corner of my home where my sun-worshipping cat, Fanny, can ascend to its highest tower and bask in sunlight all year round. My other cat, Clayton, is highly partial to crinkle balls and those little plastic toy mice with feathered tails that make a rattling sound when you shake them—a toy that costs all of about $0.99, and of which he therefore gets one or two new specimens every week.

But my cats' *real* favorite thing (aside from catnip, which I buy in a big econo-size jug once a year and distribute with a free hand) is lap-time with mom. Fanny likes to get a vigorous round of lap-based back scratching every morning, whereas Clayton insists on long, sprawling naps across my legs in the afternoons.

I'm pleased to be able to offer both in essentially unlimited quantities.

It's easy to feel that competitive spark upon seeing someone whose kids—whether those kids have four legs or two—seem to have toys and baubles and all kinds of advantages that yours simply don't and never could on your own earth-based salary.

But your fur-kids still have the single greatest advantage any fur-kid could ever have:

You for their cat-parent.

PAWSOME!

You let your cat sleep in bed with you

I've read all the so-called "experts" who say it's a bad idea to let your cats sleep in bed with you, and all I can say about that is, *phooey!*

Phooey! I say.

Living with cats and *not* letting them sleep in bed with you is about as much fun as going to the beach in a wool suit. It's about as much fun as attending school on a Saturday. It's about as much fun as taking all the singing and dancing out of *The Lion King* and turning it back into *Hamlet*.

Not that there aren't a *very* few downsides. There's waking up eyeball to...um...eyeball with the business end of a kitty tush, for example. Or sometimes finding yourself crowded off your own pillows because that's where little Trixie likes to stretch out. You may occasionally have less freedom to move your legs if your cats are snoozing at the foot of your bed. Too much jostling is likely to disturb their slumber—and lord knows it would be downright cruel to rob your moggy of even one minute out of the 960 minutes or so she spends napping each and every day.

But you'd have to be a true curmudgeon to resent any of that when it so clearly makes your cat very, *very* happy snuggle up close to you at night. She loves your warmth, your familiar smell, and the cozy feeling of being *purr*fectly protected when sleeping beside you, the only human in the whole wide world in whom she has complete and absolute trust.

As for what *you* get out of it...well...what sane person could deny that the sound of purring as you drift off to sleep is absolutely, one hundred percent

PAWSOME!

You cuddle with your cat on sick days

Years of research has consistently shown that cuddling up close to your resident feline can lower blood pressure and relieve symptoms of anxiety and depression. There's evidence that cats' purrs help broken bones mend more swiftly. Best of all, cuddle-time with cats can speed up recovery from most major and minor illnesses, including the trifling colds and flus that probably account for the majority of sick days you end up taking.

That's how cuddling with your cats on sick days benefits *you*.

From your cat's *purr*spective, your sick days are probably some of the best days around. Chances are he can't think of a single better way to pass the time than snuggling up close to you under the covers while you watch TV or read a book, or simply bask in the unaccustomed luxury of a looooooong afternoon snooze. (This is a luxury with which your cat is *highly* familiar!)

The tragedy of it (as far as your cat's concerned) is that days where you can actually remain abed for hours on end, just like your pampered puss does, probably don't come more than once or twice in a year.

But when they do come, these are great good days, indeed. Which is why the selflessness of your taking the time to make your cat soooooo happy—even in the midst of your own chest cold or sore back, or whatever else it is that's keeping you trapped in bed—is nothing short of

PAWSOME!

You let your cat snuggle between you and the arm of the chair

When it comes to comfy napping spots, probably nothing will ever be better for your cat than the coziness of a cardboard box or paper shopping bag that's just the right size—large enough to squeeze his whole body into, but small enough to feel snug and secure on all sides.

A pretty close second, though, is when your cat is able to wedge his entire body between yours and the arm of the sofa or recliner or plain old office chair you happen to be sitting in.

The warmth of it! The comforting, familiar smell of his favorite human! The feeling of being one-hundred percent safe from any and all predators who might very well be stalking your quiet, suburban neighborhood *at this very moment!*

Granted, it's not always entirely comfortable for *you.* Having a cat's body wedged between you and the arm of the couch might make it difficult to curl up in your preferred lounging position, or to use that sofa arm to prop up the book you're reading.

But how much does any of that matter? A teensy bit of discomfort is such a small price to pay, after all, for something that makes your kitty feel so very, very good.

PAWSOME!

You let your cat sleep in your favorite spot

I never really liked to share when I was a kid—not pizza or paint brushes or favorite toys.

This was especially true when it came to my personal space. As a bookish kid, I had specific little nooks and corners where I liked to curl up to read, and woe betide the playful sibling or well-meaning adult who tried to insert themselves into that space.

I was kind of selfish, is what I'm trying to say—and may well have grown from a selfish childhood into a selfish young adulthood, followed by a selfish middle age, if not for the timely intercession of the cats I first adopted in my early twenties.

I can't exactly say that my cats taught me generosity by their own big-hearted example, because cats are as territorial as any creature on the face of the earth.

It's more like they conditioned me over time, until sharing became an automatic process. Now, not only do I sit or lie someplace else—without even thinking twice!—when I happen to walk into a room and see one of my cats snoozing away in my own favorite spot, but I also smile affectionately at the sight of it.

If Childhood Me could see Adult Me, she'd be amazed at how far I've come.

PAWSOME!

You play "cat soccer" with crumpled balls of paper

Maybe you've never been much of a jock.

Maybe your participation in high school athletics is better described as "reluctant" than "record-breaking." Maybe you've had a pair of running shoes sitting next to your front door since New Year's Eve *last* year, which was when you promised yourself you'd pick up a jogging regimen that still hasn't quite materialized.

Okay, so you're not a gym rat. But that doesn't mean you can't engage with your cat in a spirited game of "cat soccer" (toss paper ball to cat, watch as cat bats paper ball around, repeat), or "throw and retrieve the plastic mouse" (knowing full well that you'll do both the throwing and the retrieving in this particular game).

Maybe your high school coach never saw you as anything more than bench-warming material. As far as your besotted kitty's concerned, however, you're first-string all the way!
PAWSOME!

You turn your floor into a minefield of garbage...er, "toys"

I used to watch that A&E show *Hoarders* with the morbid fascination of a person recognizing scenes from her own potential future.

Not that I'm a hoarder, or even much of a saver. If anything, I probably go too far in the other direction, being just as apt to discard an outdated but still wearable pair of shoes, or old boyfriends' mix tapes (who even *has* a cassette player anymore?) as I am things that are genuinely old, broken, or useless.

Nevertheless, the floors of just about every room of my house are strewn with...well...let's just call things what they are and say *garbage*. Garbage that no living soul—save for the two thoroughly spoiled feline companions who share my home—would understand the use or necessity of. Garbage that, in darker moments, I imagine some kindly intentioned cadre of professional organizers carting remorselessly away, while I stand on the sidelines wringing my hands and piteously wailing, "But I *NEED* all this stuff!"

My living room alone is a veritable minefield of straws, bottle caps, cardboard toilet-paper rolls, wads of discarded writing paper (discarded paper always being in abundant supply in a writer's house), and crumpled-up receipts that probably first entered the house in one of the many, *many* paper bags that have also taken up semi-permanent residence. And, of course, the good folks at Amazon keep us in enough variously sized cardboard boxes to outfit an army of cats.

If you're a cat lover, then chances are you have a similar story to tell about shoeboxes and ping-pong balls that linger on the floors of your home despite having long outlived their actual usefulness. And there they'll remain—creating clutter and collecting dust—even if your own aesthetic runs toward the sleek and minimalist, for no other reason than the fact that your kitties enjoy them.

Because that's just the kind of thoughtful person you are.

PAWSOME!

You turn the heater up way too high because your cat likes it toasty

C ats have managed to make their way into just about every corner of this world occupied by humans, no matter how icy or desolate some of those locales may be. Yet all cats—including snow-ready breeds like Maine Coons and Norwegian Forest cats—are descended from desert-dwelling African wild cats. And while heat is pretty much the defining characteristic of a desert, they also tend to be dangerously cold places at night.

This is all by way of explaining why, to this day, a cat's natural instinct is to soak up as much heat as possible while heat's available—the better to stockpile it against potential life-threatening night chills. This is true even if you and your cat live close to the Equator and enjoy balmy evenings all year round.

My own cat Fanny is as much a sun worshipper as her desert-dwelling ancestors ever were. And on those gray winter days when there's nary a ray of sunlight to be found, Fanny makes do with a heated cat bed resting directly in front of the giant, Nineteenth-century radiators our Nineteenth-century house came equipped with. And from there she stretches and flips over contentedly—heating first her belly, then her back, and then her belly again—all winter long.

Those giant radiators are pretty effective at warming up our drafty, high-ceilinged home. A bit *too* effective at times, actually. The desk where I do my writing sits right next to one of them, and I'll admit there are times when the heat gets to be too much for me.

Like, waaaaaay too much for me. And I'm a Florida native! Ten-year-old me used to run around outside in ninety-degree heat all summer long! So it's more than a little odd to find myself, all these years later, sweating my face off way up here in the frozen northeast while snow falls and ice puddles form outside.

It's not like I can't decrease the level of heat our radiators radiate. Mere steps from my desk is a fancy, computer-controlled wall panel that lets me do exactly that.

And yet, when I look over at Fanny and see how *very* happy all that heat makes her, I can't quite bring myself to do it.

I'll wager that most of us have made a similar decision at one time or another—the decision to endure a certain amount of physical discomfort just for the sake of making our cats happy. Not to mention, being a touch too warm during the winter months still beats the alternative.

PAWSOME!

You let your cat knead the roll above the waistband of your jeans

If you're at all like me, your physique has taken a few downward turns as you've aged out of your teens and twenties (and thirties, and...), which was probably when you last aspired to the long, lean torso that (let's face it) you now have no hope of attaining, short of an encounter with Aladdin's magic lamp.

And, maybe also like me, while you're not *embarrassed* by having a belly with a bit of a wobble, it's not like you're trying to draw everyone's attention to that fact, either.

One of the very best things about animals, and cats in particular, is how blissfully unselfconscious they are. Things that would turn you beet-red with mortification don't faze your cat in the slightest. Which is why, for example, your kitty has no second thoughts at all about planting herself smack in the middle of the living room rug while you have company over, hoisting her hind leg high in the air, and applying the cleansing scour of a raspy tongue to her nether regions with tremendous alacrity—and without the slightest twinge of embarrassment.

And which is also possibly why it never seems to occur to Ms. Mittens that you might have any feelings about that telltale roll of flesh around your midsection (one exacerbated to its fullest plumpness by the unforgiving denim waistband of your jeans) other than vicarious pleasure in the joy it gives her to knead and knead and *knead* away at it with her front paws.

It's probably the height of hypocrisy that we adore a mushy belly on a cat, yet tend to turn a disdainful eye at signs of similar mushiness in our fellow humans—a disdainful eye that we also, sadly, sometimes turn on ourselves.

Nevertheless, as a true-blue cat lover, you're more than willing to endure the emotional pain (and sometimes very real physical pain!) of having your cat remind you of this particular shortcoming while her happy little claws and paw pads work away at it.

And maybe you're even secretly kind of glad it's there—something of yourself you can offer to your cat now, in the full flush of your wise old(er) age, that you didn't have to offer in your twenties.

PAWSOME!

You sit near your cat, but not too near your cat

A ffectionate cuddling is all well and good, but everybody needs a little *purr*-sonal space sometimes, amirite? **PAWSOME!**

You overlook your cat's bad manners

C ats have a reputation for being aloof, circumspect, somewhat snooty creatures—all of which seem like incongruous things to go along with a charge of "bad manners." In fact, I can almost hear readers out there clutching their pearls and huffily exclaiming, *Bad manners??? My little Muffin??? How dare you?!*

But what else can you call it when someone, for example, takes to knocking glasses over on the coffee table for no apparent reason? Or cleans their hindquarters in public? Or yowls insistently while you're in the middle of talking to someone else? Last night, I even witnessed my cat Clayton gently place his paw in my husband's dinner plate—hoping to purloin a slice of turkey—when he thought nobody was looking.

Surely we can all agree that any human dinner guest who did such a thing would never make the Emily Post hall of fame.

The counterargument to this, naturally, is that things that seem rude to *us* are far less so when placed in the context of what might be termed "cat custom." Cat custom dictates, for example, that sniffing a newcomer's hindquarters is *good* manners. And it's not like your cat can say, "Pass the turkey."

How else is he supposed to ask for that slice sitting on your plate?

Isn't the real offense against hospitality that you didn't offer any turkey to your cat in the first place?

But just the fact that you're thinking this way when it comes to your cats' alleged breaches of etiquette indicates an acceptance of the customs of others, and alternative ways of doing things, that speaks to a certain open-mindedness on your part—an important but nevertheless rare quality, and one that's fostered by your relationship with your cat. Live and let live, you say. What's important isn't judging the nitty-gritty specific way others choose to do things like sharing food at mealtime or greeting a returned family member when she walks in the door. It's the fact that they choose to do those things with *us* that matters.

If there were more people like you, the world would be an infinitely better place!

PAWSOME!

You let your cat climb you like a tree trunk

N ot every cat's a climber, but the ones who are *really* love to climb. They'll clamber up the drapes, claw their way up the side of the couch, and scramble to the tippy top of their cat tree, where they'll pose triumphantly atop the very highest perch. I've even seen a determined cat ascend all the way to the top of a completely vertical, seven-foot bookcase (and then have no earthly idea how to get back down).

Climbing is a behavior that's evolutionarily hardwired into cats. Felines in the wild are both predator and prey, and trees are not only handy hiding spots—the better from which to launch surprise attacks while simultaneously remaining out of reach of their own would-be attackers—they also offer enough height to allow a cat to survey the terrain for miles around.

Your kitty doesn't need to worry about such things, of course. But much like humans, who no longer need to run from lions and mammoths but who now run for fun, many indoor cats still get a kick out of scaling to the highest heights your home has to offer.

But it's not just the destination that matters. That journey to the top is fun all on its own. And what could be more fun for your frisky feline than using *you*, her beloved and devoted slave, as a human tree trunk? Why not employ your denim-clad legs as a handy shortcut to the kitchen counter? (So much more entertaining than jumping straight from the floor!) And if it's your shoulder that's the goal—some cats having a fondness for riding around on human shoulders the way Indian rajas once rode in on elephants—then climbing directly up your legs just makes sense.

Of course, the main difference between you and an actual tree trunk is that a tree's bark is significantly tougher than human flesh. Your fluffy little kitty's surprisingly sharp claws probably do a lot more damage to you than they would to a tree's rough skin.

Sometimes love is pain. That's why you take it like a champ!
PAWSOME!

You wake up early, even on your days off, to feed your cat

C hances are you think of yourself, at least occasionally, as someone who works hard to give her cat a better life.

Your cats enjoy all the playtime they want, and that's because most of *your* time is spent toiling away for a boss who's kind of a jerk, alongside coworkers who don't quite rise to the level of oddball camaraderie depicted on *The Office*. Hopefully, though, you have a couple of days off in the typical week, when you can hypothetically sleep well into the early afternoon if you feel like it. (And if you're still young enough to be able to sleep that late. Ah, the things I failed to appreciate when I was in my twenties!)

I'm an early riser, myself. Mostly I wake up early to get to work, because even we self-employed writer types have to deal with deadlines, and work-related emails, and tasks assigned by the people we answer to, and things to check over from the people who answer to us.

Even on my days off, though, I'd never dream of lying in bed more than twenty minutes (at most!) past my usual time. And that's because my cats' bellies—much like *all* cats' bellies—never take a day off. It could be six a.m. on a deadline day when I have to get pages to my editor no later than seven...or it could be six a.m. on Christmas Day, when absolutely nobody I work with wants to hear from me.

Either way, if I'm not awake and at least alert enough to trudge downstairs and dump some food into a bowl, there's going to be hell to pay. As the old adage goes, there's no snooze button on a hungry cat.

Your friends who don't have cats probably feel some combination of pity and smugness when they hear tales of your early-morning wakeups in service of your four-legged bestie. *Imagine getting up THAT early just to feed a cat!*

And, sure, they may have a point. But those poor saps will also never know the joys of waking up to the sound of purring on the pillow next to their head, to the feeling of a little pink nose booping their own, to the delightful shiver of a single velvety paw brushing against their cheek, creating that tiny moment of intense love and fulfilment before they have to face the grim realities of the day.

Most of all, they'll never know how great it feels to begin each and every day by providing complete happiness and satisfaction to another living soul—accomplished with no more difficulty than a mere flick of the wrist and a pop-top can of cat food.

PAWSOME!

You hang out with your cat, doing nothing but enjoying each other's company

These are some of the very best moments of your own life.

And as for how your cat feels about them?
Sheer and utter *purr*fection!
PAWSOME!

You let your cat explore the deep, dark recesses of closets, cabinets, and drawers

C ats are famously curious creatures, and curiosity all on its own would be ample justification for your kitty's longing to explore all the nooks and crannies of your closets, cabinets, and drawers—darkly mysterious treasure troves of moldering old shoe boxes or tempting morsels of spilled foods.

Chances are you have one cat in particular who's especially fond of dark corners. In our home, that cat is Fanny. I once (this is a true story) spent quite some time saving up for a ridiculously expensive and thoroughly impractical pair of boots that I nonetheless coveted with an unholy lust. Having finally procured them, I stored them in their accompanying dust bag deep in the back of my closet...only to find, when I went to put them on for the first time some two months later, that Fanny had left a series of tiny raised claw marks all over the leather upper of one of the boots.

I can only blame myself, I suppose, for not having remembered that a) Fanny likes to spend a good chunk of her daily hours buried in the closet and b) the boots' dust bag—while unfailingly protecting them from dust—was never likely to offer much protection from a set of persistent claws.

The lesson I gleaned from this incident wasn't that I should keep my cats out of the closet—rather, it was that I should keep anything I valued on a high-enough shelf that the cats wouldn't be able to reach it.

How could I keep my cats out of my closets, anyway? Or from napping atop a pricey pile of cashmere sweaters in an open drawer? I mean, I know *how*, of course—being, despite ample evidence to the contrary, bright enough to understand how a locked door or closed drawer would be capable of physically repelling a cat's attempt to get at the goodies inside.

What I mean is, how could I bring myself to do it? How could any of us?

Loving a cat means looking for ways to make them happy. Even if making them happy means occasionally letting them play Lewis and Clark in your pantry or in the back of your closet.

Even if making them happy means sometimes allowing them to spelunk in the depths of your sock drawer.

Even if making them happy means sacrificing a super-cool pair of boots that you really, really, *really* wanted.

It's all right, though. Everybody knows that people who live to make others happy are totally and completely
PAWSOME!

You spoil your cats rotten

My husband isn't especially difficult to figure out—an attribute that I note here with a great deal of approval. Cats are hard enough to understand without throwing an excessively complicated human housemate into the mix.

Still, there are times when he manages to leave me completely befuddled. Like when he walks into the living room and finds me on the couch with a velvet cushion on my lap, atop which my cat Clayton is sprawled on his back while I give him a thorough tummy rub, and he will say (my husband, that is) with a clear note of disapproval in his voice:

"You spoil these cats rotten."

It's not the observation itself that leaves me so perplexed. Of *course* I spoil my cats rotten. That I do so is an inarguable fact. I spoil them absolutely and unapologetically, and if I have any single regret about it at all, it would only be that I'm not creative enough to come up with even more ways of spoiling them rotten-er. (Suggestions are always welcomed! @ me on Instagram!)

It's the disapproval in my husband's tone that I can't quite grok. I mean, what's even the *point* of adopting a cat—particularly a rescue cat—if it *isn't* to spoil them rotten???

Nevertheless, this self-evident observation is one that's oft repeated in our home. "You're spoiling them," my husband informs me, when I come home from the pet store with an entire shopping bag filled with brand-new catnip toys. "I can't believe how spoiled these cats are," he says ,whenever I prepare little Thanksgiving plate of food for the cats, so they can celebrate along with us. "These are the most ridiculously spoiled cats I've ever seen in my life," he'll insist while watching me cede half my pillow at night to a fuzzy sleeping companion. (Forgetting, perhaps, that the only other cats he's ever spent much time with were the three cats I had when we first moved in together seventeen years ago—three cats who were, I can assure you, just as spoiled then as my current cats are today.)

Sometimes I have to lean in and listen closely to hear his expressions of disapproval, like when I'm in the grocery store carefully evaluating varieties of Temptation treats in order to make sure I only bring home my cats' preferred flavors, while my husband stands next to me shaking his head and muttering, "It is *unbelievable* how spoiled these cats are."

Occasionally I wonder what he thinks is the potential downside of spoiling our cats. Does he worry that I'm not raising them right? That I'm fostering feline narcissism? That when they go out into the world and have to cope with friends and spouses and bosses, they'll be socially maladapted or have unrealistic perceptions of their own importance?

What *exactly* is the harm?

And does my husband honestly think I don't know what's what when I see him coming home with some fancy can of high-end tuna he knows they like, or when he slips Clayton little bits of the turkey from the sandwich he's just made himself, or when—after he thinks I've fallen asleep next to him—he gives Fanny the long and intense late-night back-scratches she craves, while murmuring in her ear, *Who's my pretty girl? Who's a pretty, pretty girl?*

The truth is, there are plenty of people in the world who are selfish or stingy or downright cruel. They're the ones who tend to make the world a worse place to live in. But there are also a handful of us kicking around this big blue marble who take a profound pleasure in making others happy.

And while the business of making other *people* happy (although unquestionably worthwhile!) can be immensely complicated, making a cat happy is usually a much simpler affair—easily accomplished with plentiful chin scritches, a bagful of crunchy treats, and a few strategically placed cushions in sunlit spots around the house.

PAWSOME!

You will never leave your cat

Over the course of a lifetime, you'll leave homes and schools and jobs and lovers. You'll leave friends you swore you'd never forget and restaurants you used to eat in once a week and at least one teacher who changed your life forever. You'll leave behind yearbooks and schoolbooks and old toys and broken appliances and furniture you spent hours and hours shopping for and shoes that are no longer fashionable and the wildly patterned dishes you bought back when you first got your own place, but that now don't seem quite like "you."

But the one thing you will never—*ever*—leave behind is your cat.

You will never outgrow your cat. You will never try to upgrade your old cat with a newer model. You will never decide that whereas cats used to be all the rage—everybody on TikTok has one!—now they're passé.

You will never ditch your cat because life has gotten too hard or too complicated or too much fun in ways that would make it easier not to have the obligation of caring for a cat. You will never move away and leave your cat behind because moving with a cat is inconvenient, or because you've decided to begin a new life somewhere else, or because maybe you're moving in with someone who doesn't like cats all that much.

How would that even work, anyway? Your cat is your heart, after all. And everybody knows it's impossible to go off somewhere and starat anew while leaving your heart behind.

You'd never even think of trying.

PAWSOME!

You love your cats the way they are

E very cat has their own distinct personality, as any cat lover will tell you. I once lived with a cat who found it intensely unbearable to be in the presence of any human being other than me. At the other end of the spectrum, one of the cats I live with now is so very desperate for human attention that he actually likes going to the vet's office—*where they give him shots*—because at least the person administering the shots is paying attention to him while doing so.

There are cats as happy as the day is long, and cats whose primary personality trait is hostility. There are playful cats and there are prissy cats. There are cats who like to lie in laps, cats who prefer to be lap-adjacent (not so much *on* as *near* their preferred human), and then there are cats who'd rather nap solo. There are cats who love eating "people food," and cats content to stick with their own kibble, thank you very much.

If we're being totally honest, we have to admit that certain qualities are probably objectively better than others. It's better to have a cat who purrs for guests than a cat who's a biter. It's better to have a cat who tolerates the other cats in your house, or who's friendly to the significant other you recently committed to, or who uses the litterbox—and *only* the litter-box—when nature calls.

But, nevertheless...

Ask somebody why they love the person they love, and you're apt to hear things like, "She's smart. She's funny. She's a good friend to her friends." And, sure, those are all legitimate reasons to admire someone.

Here's the great truth when it comes to love, however: While you can always point to the reasons, the reasons aren't the point.

This was a fundamental truth I never fully understood until I came to live with cats and got to know other cat lovers. In twenty-five years, I've never heard a single one say something like, "I love my Buttons because she's so friendly," or "I love Snowflake because he's so playful."

The truth is, we don't love our cats because of specific personality traits they may or may not possess. We love our cats simply because they're ours.

Which is really just another way of saying that cat lovers have been gifted with a tremendous capacity for love—a love that doesn't judge, that doesn't demand, and that doesn't bother trying to look for quasi-logical explanations that don't even matter all that much, anyway.

PAWSOME!

You're your cat's voice and his champion

W hat would your cat do without you?

Who loves your cat like you love him? Who knows your cat like you know him? Who else knows that he's terrified by the sound of a plastic trash bag snapping open? Or that a small, nondescript stuffed worm with a bell in its tail has been his best friend and very favorite toy ever since he was a kitten? Or that, when his tummy's upset, adding a little canned pumpkin to his food is the only thing that makes him feel better?

Nobody—that's who.

Without being too dramatic about it, it's probably fair to say that your love is the only thing standing between your cat and the tender mercies of a frequently cruel world. You're the one who speaks up if a visiting friend's playful children are roughhousing with Buttons a little *too* enthusiastically. And if that too-aggressive play leads your cat to retaliate with a scratch or two, it's you who will speak up in his defense and try to explain what happened from his point of view. *He was trying to tell you he'd had enough when his tail got puffy.*

Scratching and biting are imperfect communications tools, at best—but your cat only uses these tools for lack of any other ability to convey his needs, fears, or desires.

That's where you come in.

The need to act as your cat's interpreter and defender is apt to spring up unexpectedly, in unforeseen ways. You might end up with a significant other who doesn't quite understand or get along with your cat at first. You might have a neighbor who thinks your cat meows too loudly at night and complains to your landlord about it. You might have an exceptionally tidy roommate who doesn't understand *why* there have to be empty paper shopping bags right in the middle of your living room floor.

I've seen three cats through end-of-life illnesses. In each case, their doctor prescribed courses of treatment of varying aggressiveness. Doctors are experts, of course, and their expertise is what we pay them for.

But while a doctor may be an expert on the subject of medical care in general, only *you* are an expert when it comes to your cat. I was ultimately the one who had to consider each recommendation our doctor made in light of the cat that recommendation was for. And I was the one who had to push back when a cat let me know—in ways that were unmistakable, but that nevertheless only I could understand—when that course of treatment was more than the cat in question could handle.

And then I had to do what everybody reading this has had to do for their own cat at some point. I had to find my voice—and I had to use it.

Speaking up to contradict a doctor, or standing up to a significant other, or telling off a roommate or a friend can be difficult. And it's completely understandable if it's the kind of thing you have a hard time finding the courage to do on your own behalf.

When it comes to your cat, though?

You're a gladiator.

You're Braveheart.

You're a downright, honest-to-gosh, take-no-prisoners warrior-hero.

PAWSOME!

You find the strength to let your cat go when it's time

And it is—one-hundred percent—the hardest thing you will ever, ever do.

Never doubt for a moment how strong you are for doing it.

PAWSOME

You do thoughtful and completely selfless things for your cat

I've given it the old college try, but the truth is that no one book could ever truly capture all the manifold and wonderful things you do to make your cat's life just a little bit better on a daily basis.

We've gotten all the way to the end of this book, after all, without even talking about things like how you clean your cat's eyes when they get goopy, or trim their nails (which would otherwise become overgrown and painful) even when they fight you, or pull ticks and burrs—and the occasional wayward price sticker—from their fur, or go to three different stores just to track down that one hard-to-find brand of food they really love.

We couldn't begin to cover in a single book all the times you spontaneously buy your cat a new toy while you're out shopping for other things, or accept with good nature the scratches that your kitty's overly enthusiastic playtimes or cuddle sessions sometimes leave on your hands, or ditch the friends or lovers who say unkind things about your cats that your cats may never hear, but that nonetheless rankle in your own loyal and steadfast heart.

Some of the things you do and the sacrifices you make are huge—like when you forgo that badly needed new pair of shoes so you can pay your cat's medical bills. Some of them are the kinds of small, run-of-the-mill things that are so rarely noticed—like whispering softly in your kitty's ear when she has a bad dream—that nonetheless make up the very substance of a life with someone you love.

But whether they're large or small, difficult or easy, once-in-a-lifetime or thoroughly ordinary, never doubt for a moment that even if loving your cat like you do doesn't change the world, it does make the world an infinitely better place for that one little cat.

Actually, scratch that: Making the world better for one little cat is precisely the kind of thing that—were everyone to do it the way you do—*would* make the whole world better for all of us.

But you already knew that.

PAWSOME!

THE HILARIOUS NEXT INSTALLMENT IN THE "PAWSOME" SERIES!

PAWSOME!
HEAD BONKS, RASPY TONGUES, AND 101 REASONS WHY CATS MAKE US SO, SO HAPPY

GWEN COOPER
NEW YORK TIMES BESTSELLING AUTHOR OF HOMER'S ODYSSEY

"Yet another wonderful book from Gwen Cooper! If you love cats, you will love PAWSOME! It's full of furry love, fun, humor, and everything wonderful."
--Amazon Reviewer

————— ✳ —————

The *purr*fect treat for the cat lover in your life--or for yourself!

CAT BOOKS FOR CAT LOVERS!

Be sure to check out more of *New York Times* bestselling
author Gwen Cooper's celebrated books for cat
lovers—including tales of her real-life feline family and the
world-famous Homer the Blind Wonder Cat!

Get a FREE copy of the book
Homer Returns:
More True Tales of a Blind Wonder Cat & His Fur Family
Visit www.gwencooper.com

Heartfelt thanks and profound gratitude to the following people (and cats!), without whom I could never have completed this book.

Special thanks to Patti, Nikolaka & Koa!

- » Alyson Amsterdam (and Louie & Biggie)
- » Margaret Auld-Louie (and Julius & Simba)
- » Jamery Sue Barry (and Colby, Sully, Misty & Georgie)
- » Charles Brackney (and Shane, Chloe & Abby)
- » Julie Burns
- » Lisa Calarese (and Riley, Mordecai & Rigby)
- » Deborah Foresman (and Tinkerbell)
- » Paul Froiland (and Louie & Fitzy)
- » Meg Galipault (and Scout, Waffles, Sisu, Dru & Huckleberry)
- » Lee-Ann Gilliam
- » Tracy Ginnane
- » Wanda Goodwin (and Lewie Stewart)
- » Jill Graves
- » Susan Haenicke (and Bessie & Hamilton)

» Marianne Harding (and Charles Carlos Ambrose Harding)
» J. Eric Hoehn
» Susan Anne Kadlec
» Julie Kennedy
» Connie Keith-Kerns (and Zoey, Ari Kai & Mrf)
» Calvin & Eileen Keyser (and Ashes, Ninja & Snickers)
» Beth Kirby
» Ken Kistner
» Ronald Koltnow (and Speedy)
» Catherine Larklund
» Louisa Lee
» Carole Loftin (and Sadie, Biscuit & Brazil)
» Julie Lowe (and Gracie, Cougar, Java, Raven, Meeko, & Bella)
» Neta Mercer (and Pouncer, Felix & Snacks)
» TJ Murphy (and Shelly, Max, Gio & Anna)
» David Nagreski (and Chassis)
» Matthew O'Leary (and Hank)
» Melanie Paradise (and Idia)
» Stephanie Peters (and Max)
» D.H. Powell IV (and Bobby & Willow)
» Vanessa Ramirez
» Stephanie Reicen (and Oliver, Mickey & Helen)
» Kathryn Rigsby
» Felicia Roe (and Eurydice & Cassiopeia)
» Janice Rogenski
» Kathy Schlichthernlein (and Scrappy & the Gang)
» Zoe Shinno (and Midnite)
» Christine Sorenson
» Emily Stafford (and Randy & Pepper)
» Anne Teghtmeyer

» Lenai Waite (and Martin)
» Allison Walls (and Podo, Rue & Dom)
» Katie Williams
» Michele Zarichny

Printed in Great Britain
by Amazon